35 CHRISTMAS SONGS & CAROLS

featuring
WE NEED A LITTLE CHRISTMAS
from the Broadway Musical "MAME"

Arranged by
MARTINELLI

CONTENTS

Cover Photo: John Gajda

A publication of
MPL COMMUNICATIONS, INC.

EXCLUSIVELY DISTRIBUTED BY
HAL•LEONARD CORPORATION
7777 W. BLUEMOUND RD. P.O. BOX 13819 MILWAUKEE, WI 53213

2

THE CHRISTMAS SONG
(Chestnuts Roasting On An Open Fire)

Words and Music by
MEL TORMÉ
and ROBERT WELLS

Slowly

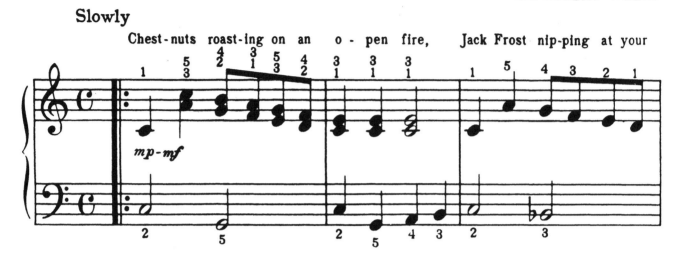

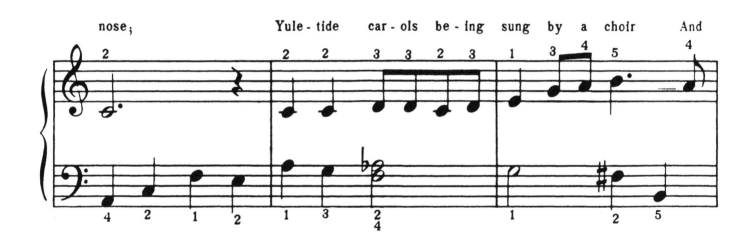

4

THE BIRTHDAY OF A KING

W. H. NEIDLINGER

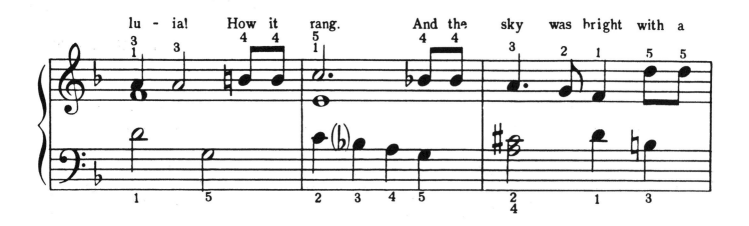

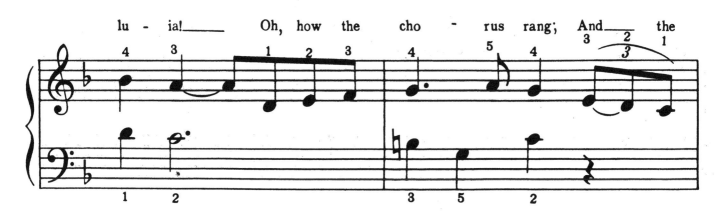

sky was bright with a ho - ly light, 'Twas THE

BIRTH - DAY OF A 1. KING. 2. 'Twas a 2. KING.

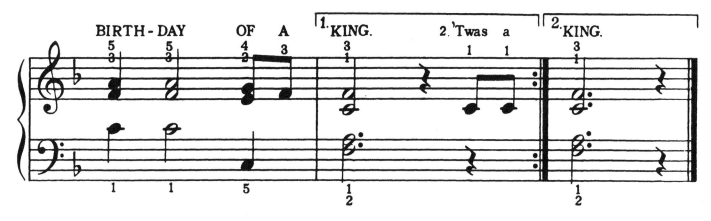

O, HOLY NIGHT
(Cantique De Noel)

ADOLPHE ADAM

Slow

O HO - LY NIGHT, the stars are bright-ly shin - ing, It is the

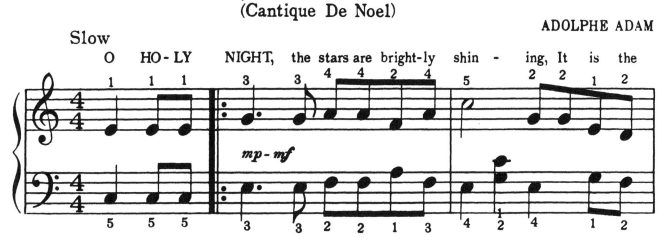

mp - mf

night of the dear Sav - iour's birth.   Long lay the

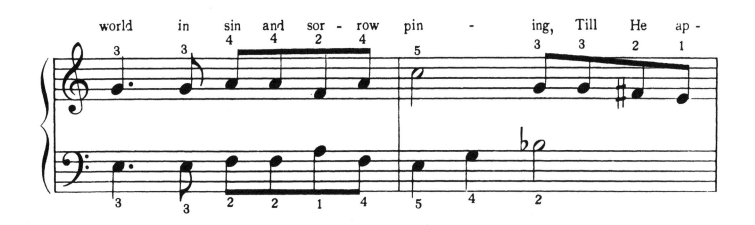

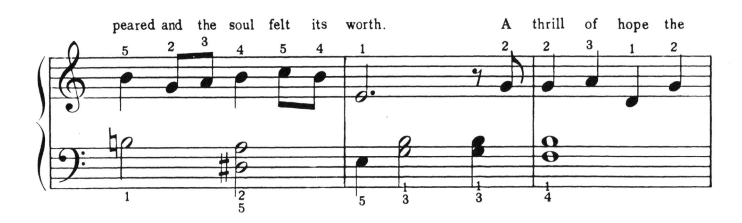

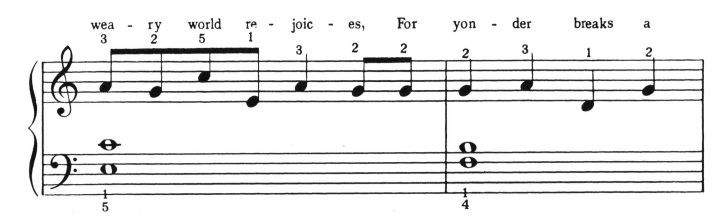

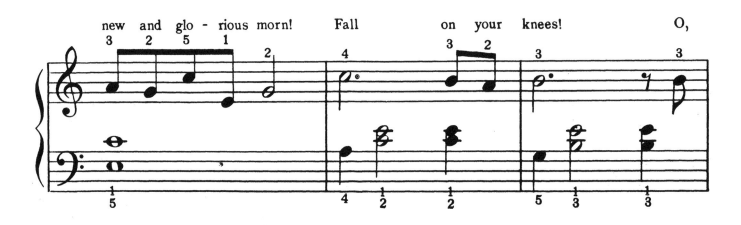

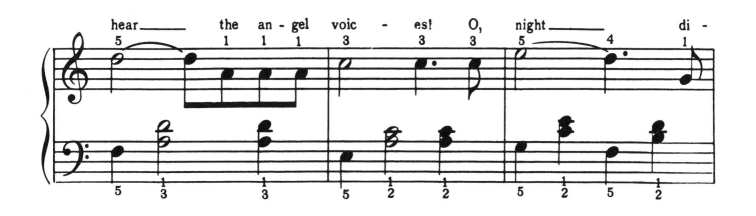

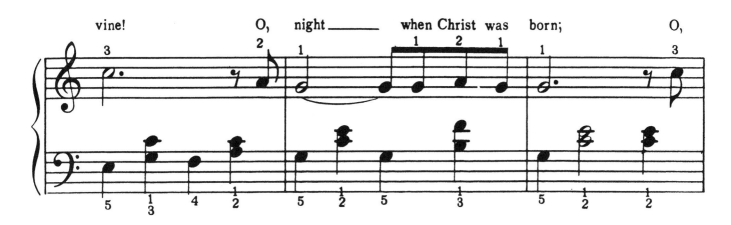

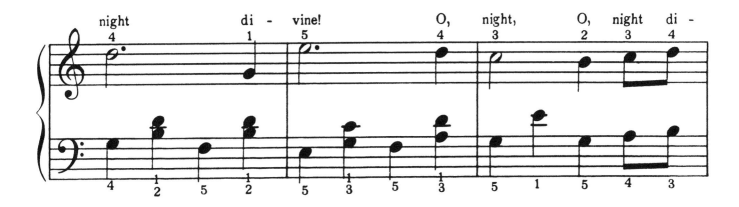

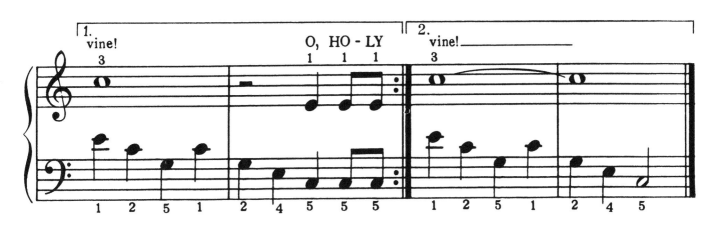

STAR OF THE EAST

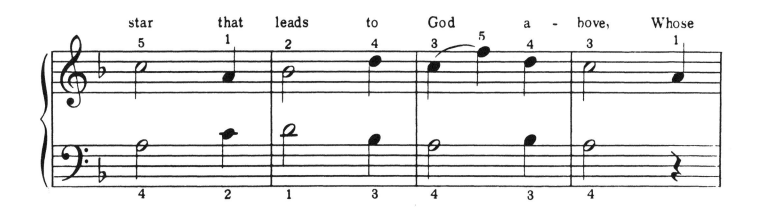

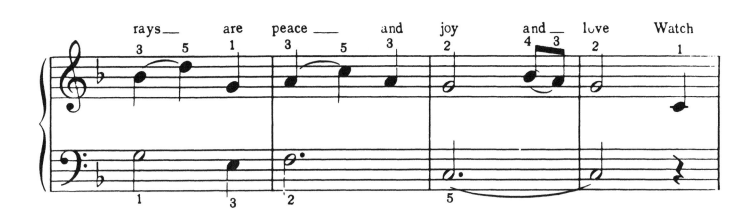

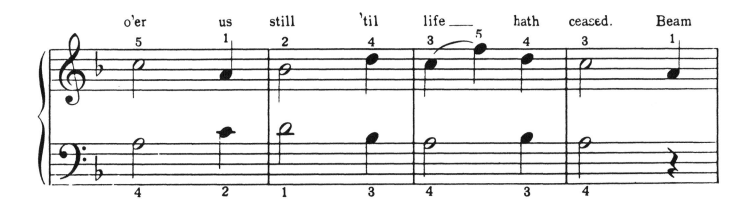

GOOD CHRISTIAN MEN REJOICE

GOD REST YOU, MERRY GENTLEMEN

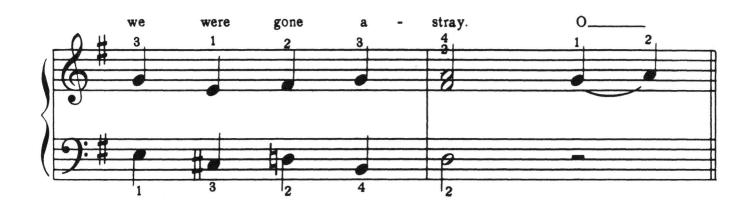

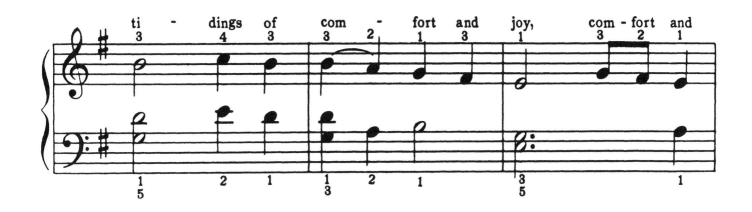

O CHRISTMAS TREE!
(O Tannenbaum)

English Text by
FLORENCE MARTIN

Old German

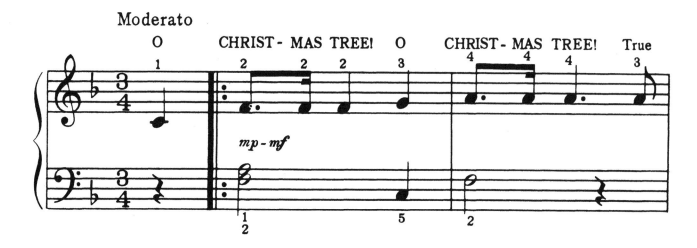

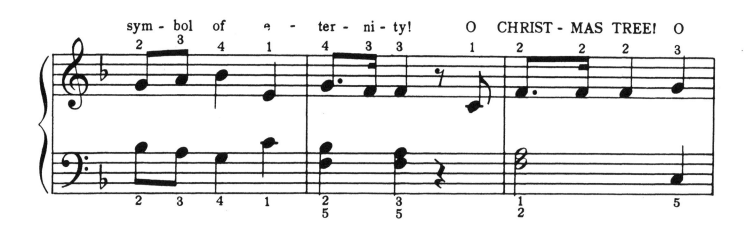

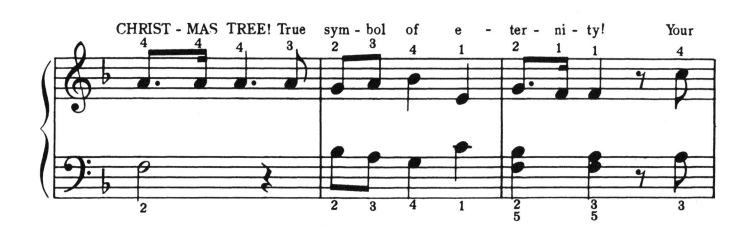

DECK THE HALLS WITH BOUGHS OF HOLLY

Moderately

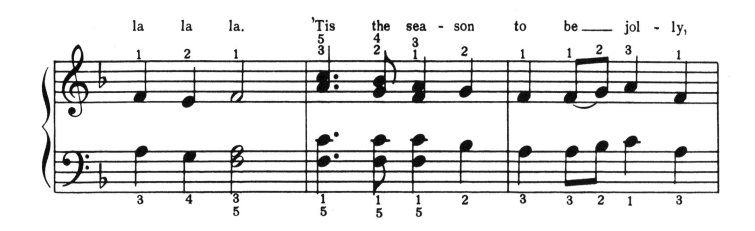

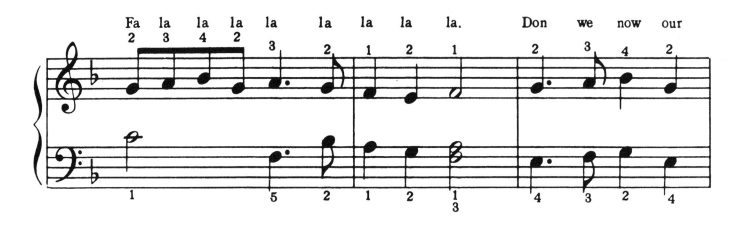

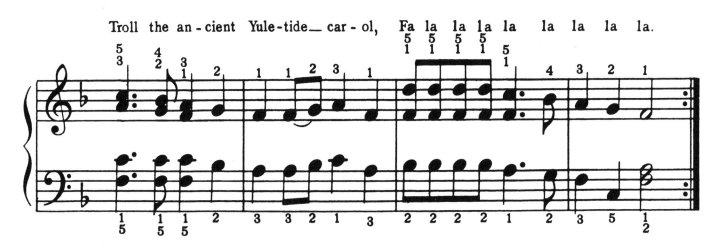

IT CAME UPON THE MIDNIGHT CLEAR

EDMUND H. SEARS

RICHARD S. WILLIS

ANGELS WE HAVE HEARD ON HIGH

Moderato

A MERRY AMERICAN CHRISTMAS

GLADYS SHELLEY

RUTH CLEARY

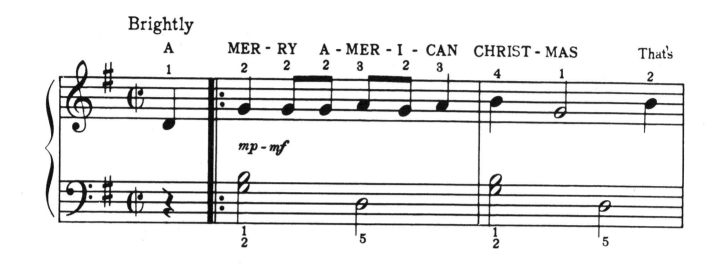

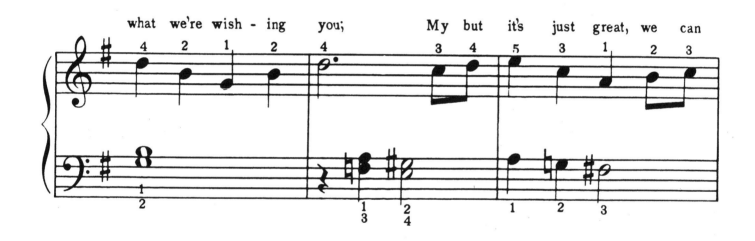

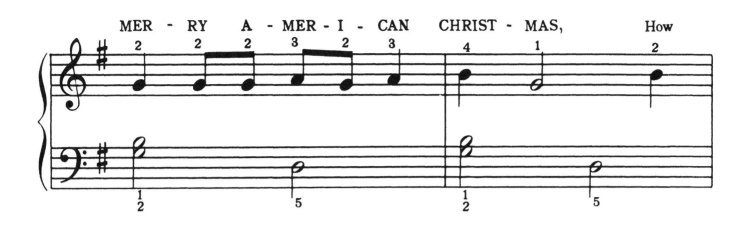

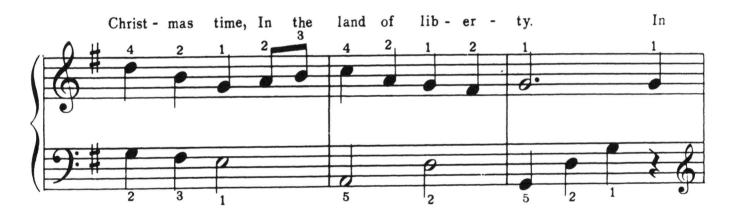

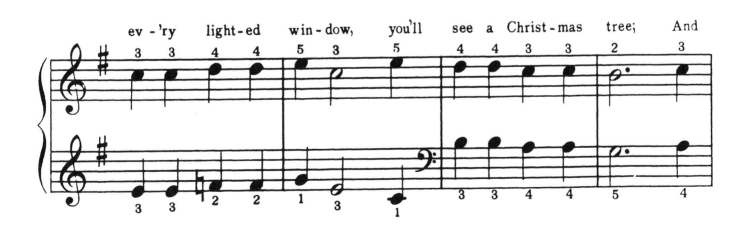

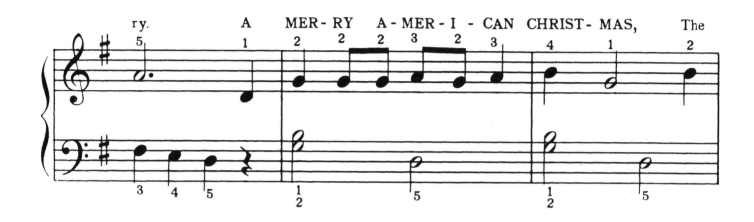

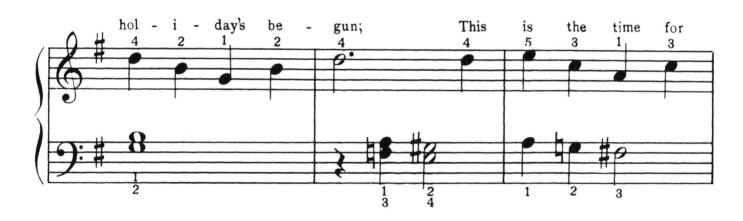

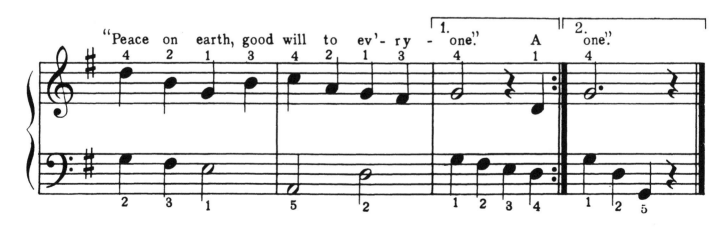

I SAW THREE SHIPS

SHEPHERDS! SHAKE OFF YOUR DROWSY SLEEP

WE WISH YOU A MERRY CHRISTMAS

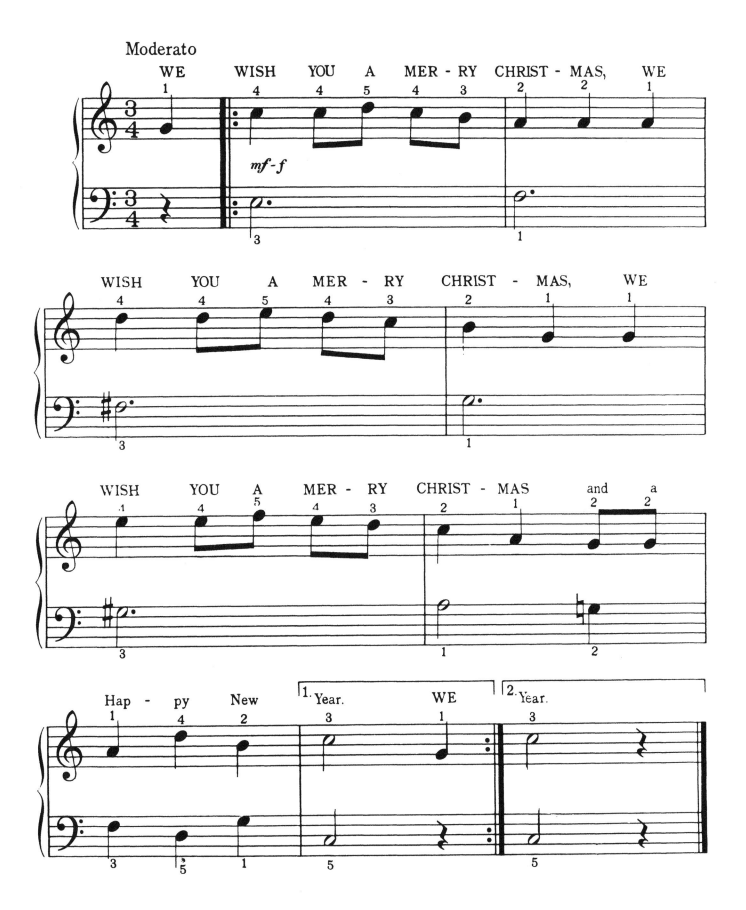

MERRY CHRISTMAS TO YOU!
HAPPY NEW YEAR TO YOU!

William Stickles

O LITTLE TOWN OF BETHLEHEM

PHILLIPS BROOKS

LEWIS H. REDNER

JOY TO THE WORLD

ISAAC WATTS

HANDEL

LUTHER'S CRADLE HYMN

MARTIN LUTHER

CARL MULLER

THE FIRST NOWELL

JOLLY OLD ST. NICHOLAS

GOOD KING WENCESLAS

I HEARD THE BELLS ON CHRISTMAS DAY

SANTA CLAUS FOR PRESIDENT!

PETER TINTURIN

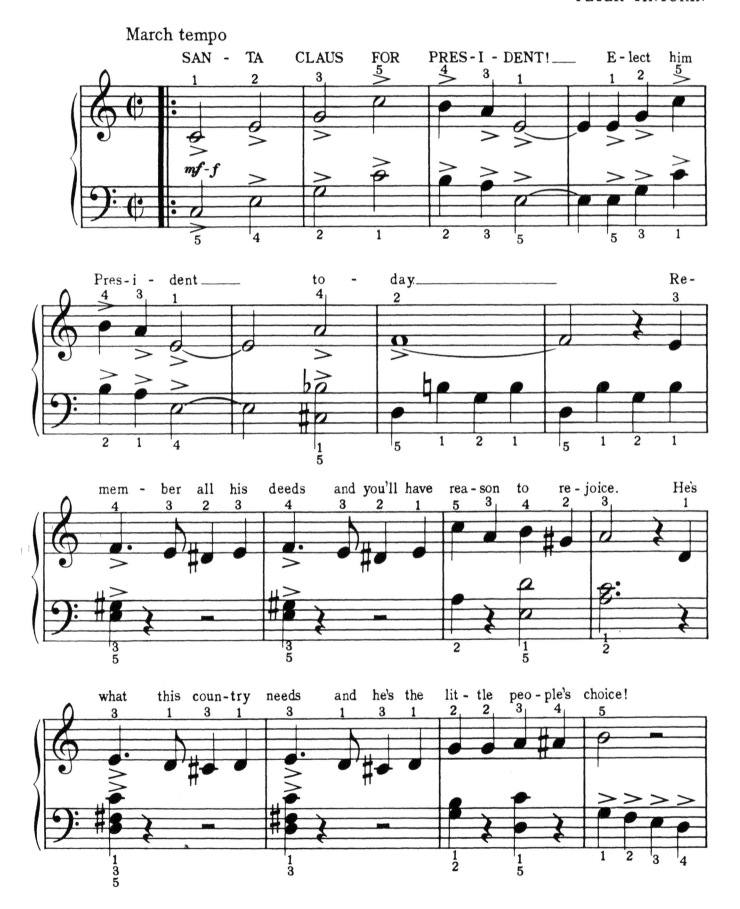

O COME, ALL YE FAITHFUL
(Adeste Fideles)

Tr. CANON FREDERICK OAKLEY, 1802

"Adeste Fideles"
J. READING

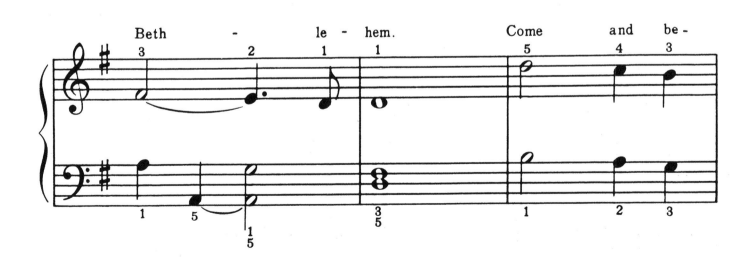

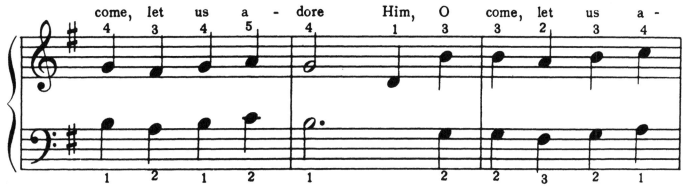

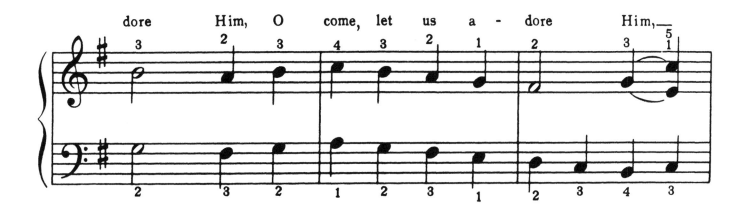

O Come etc.-2

WONDERFUL CHRISTMASTIME

Words and Music by
McCARTNEY

Brightly

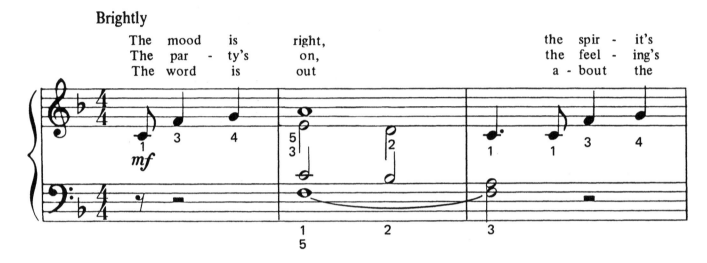

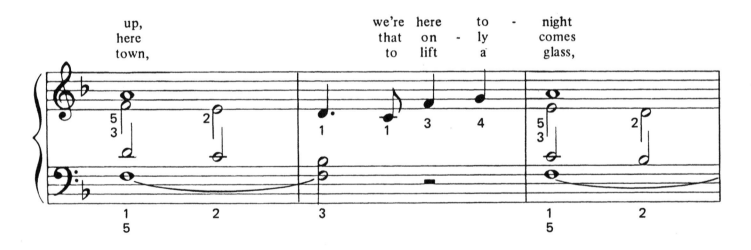

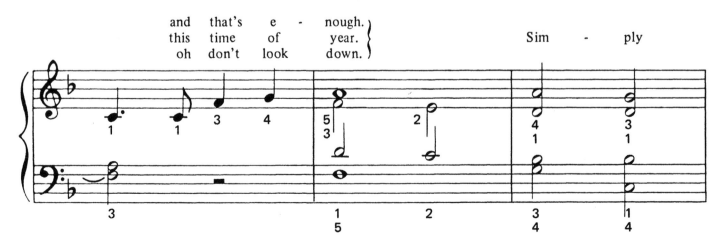

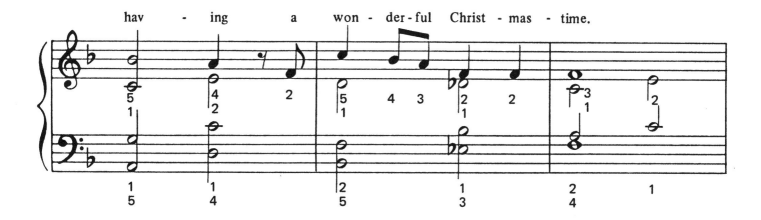

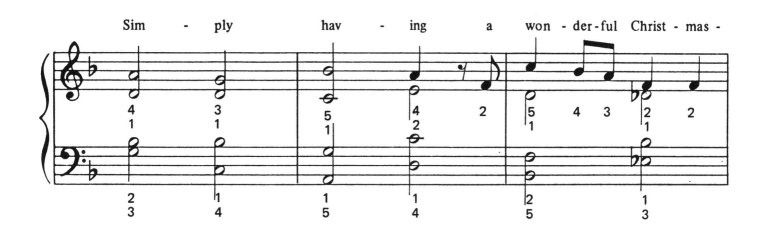

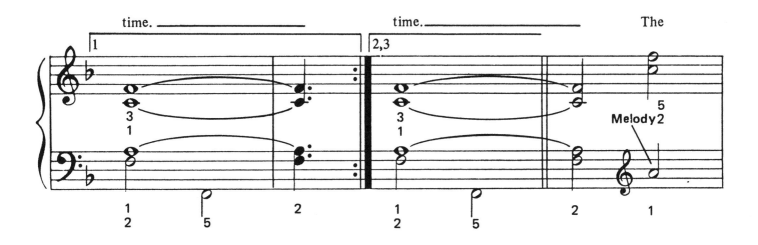

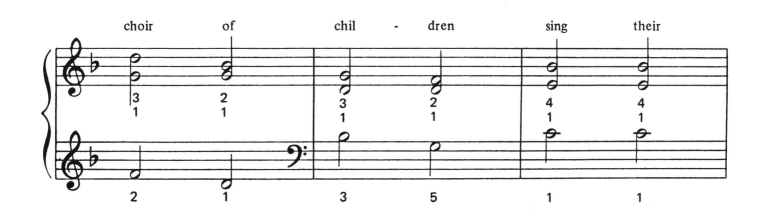

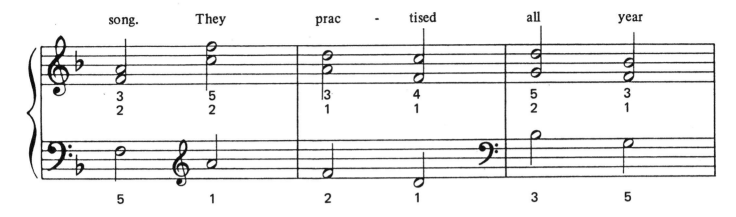

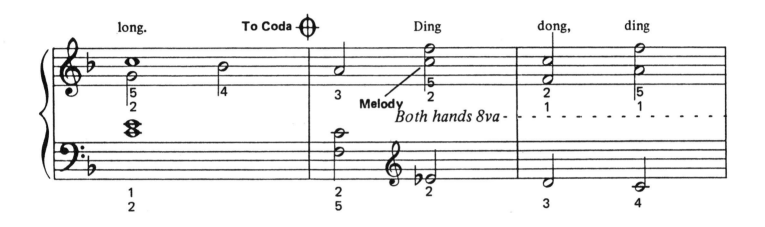

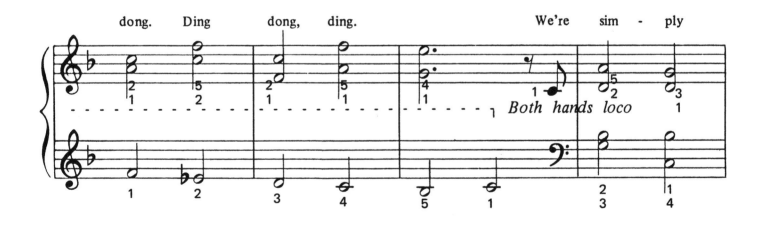

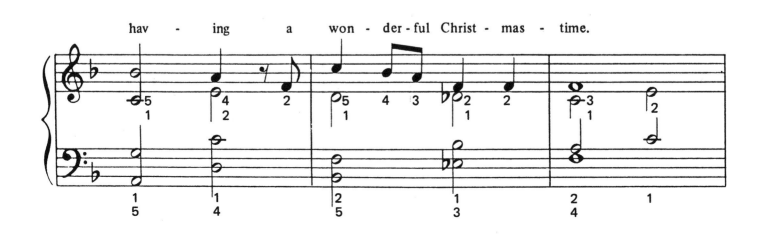

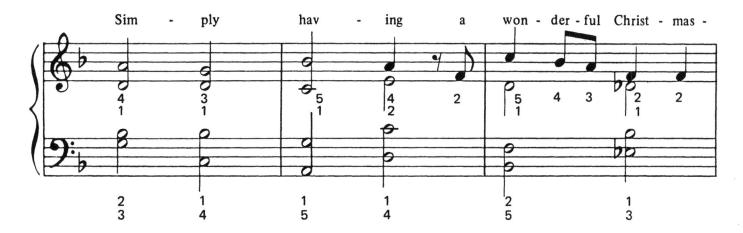

Sim - ply hav - ing a won - der - ful Christ - mas -

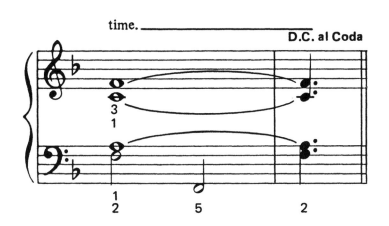

time. _____ D.C. al Coda

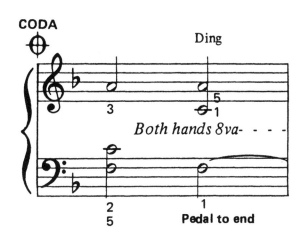

CODA

Ding

Both hands 8va- - - - -

Pedal to end

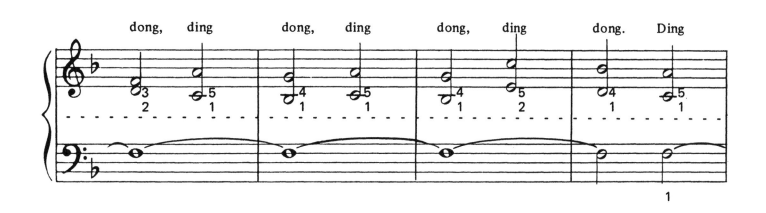

dong, ding dong, ding dong, ding dong. Ding

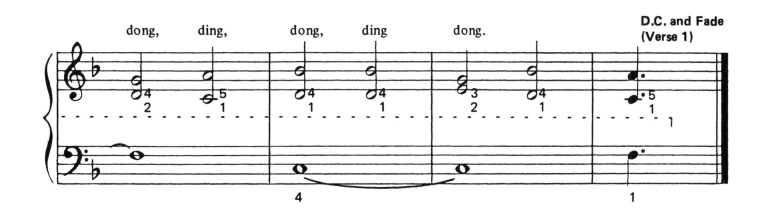

dong, ding, dong, ding dong.

D.C. and Fade
(Verse 1)

LET'S HAVE AN OLD FASHIONED CHRISTMAS

LARRY CONLEY

JOE SOLOMON

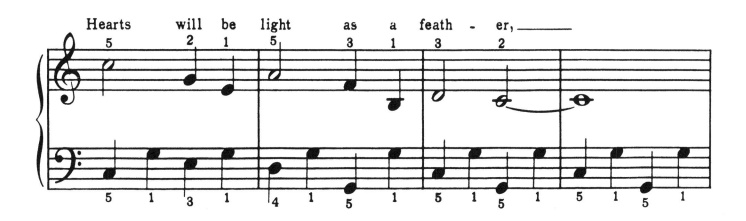

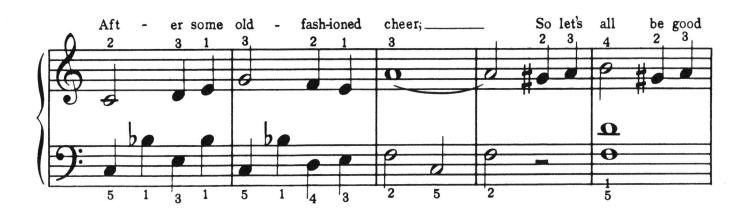

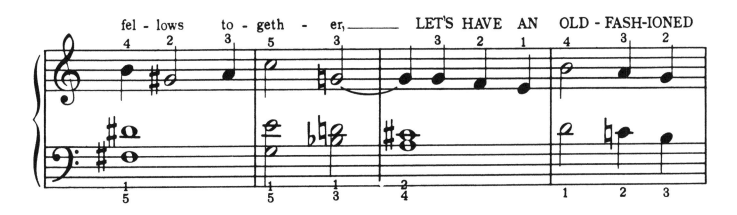

MISTER SANTA

PAT BALLARD

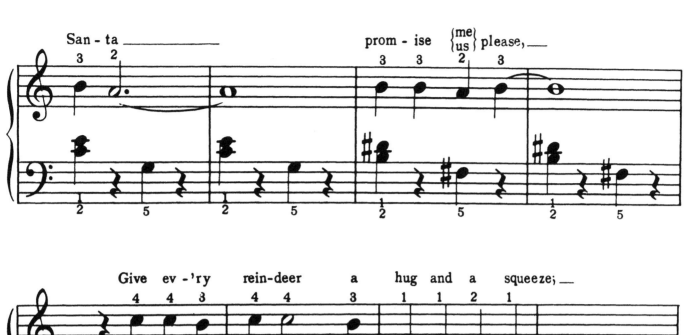

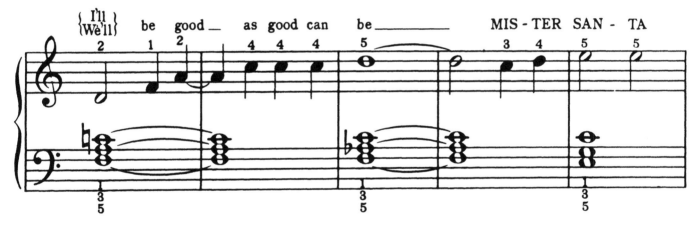

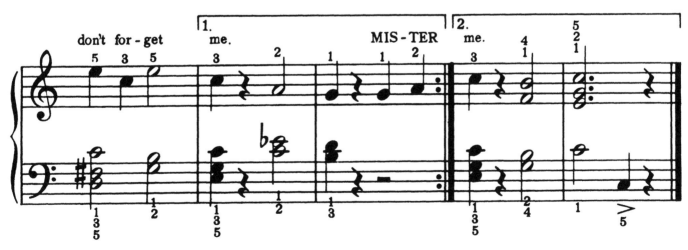

HARK! THE HERALD ANGELS SING

FELIX MENDELSSOHN

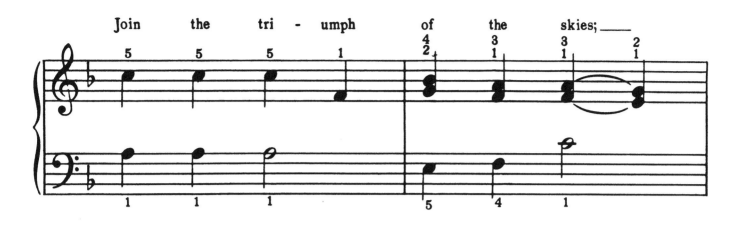

Join   the   tri - umph   of   the   skies; ___

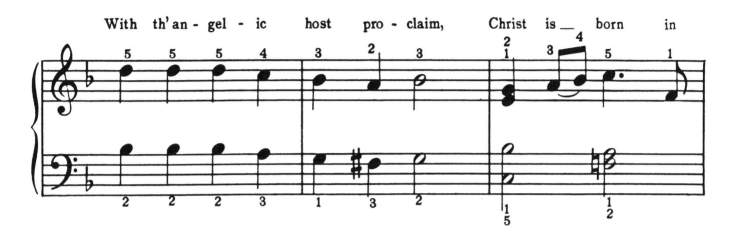

With th'an - gel - ic   host pro - claim,   Christ is __ born   in

Beth - le - hem.   HARK! THE HER - ALD   AN - GELS SING,

Glo - ry ___ to   the   new - born   King.

AWAY IN A MANGER

MARTIN LUTHER

J. E. SPILMAN

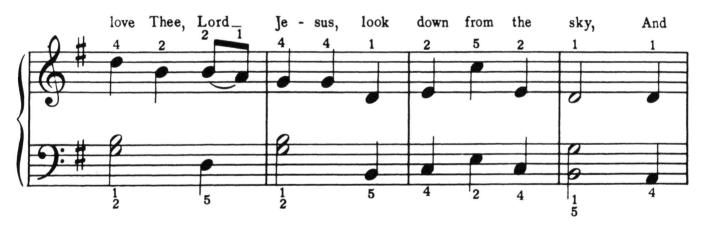

WE THREE KINGS OF ORIENT ARE

J. H. HOPKINS

THE WASSAIL SONG
(Christmas Or New Year)

JINGLE BELLS

J. PIERPONT

TELL SANTY I LIVE IN A SHANTY

HARRY PEASE

BILLY HAID

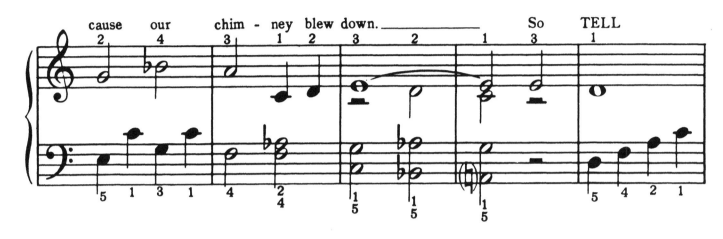

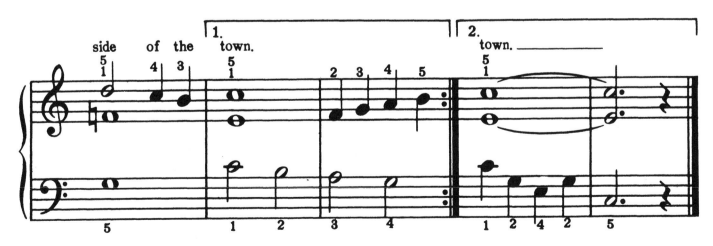

From The Broadway Musical "MAME"

WE NEED A LITTLE CHRISTMAS

Music and Lyric by
JERRY HERMAN

Bright Polka Tempo

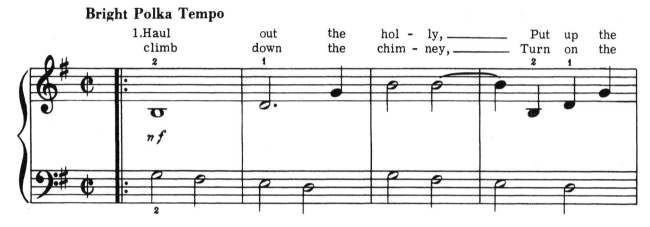

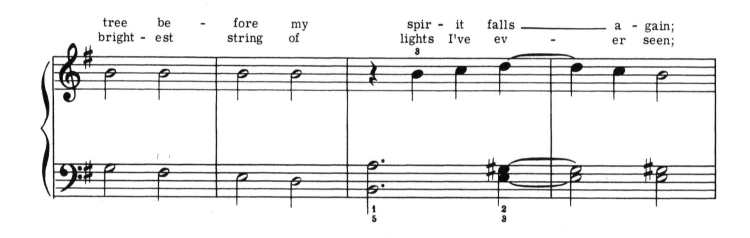

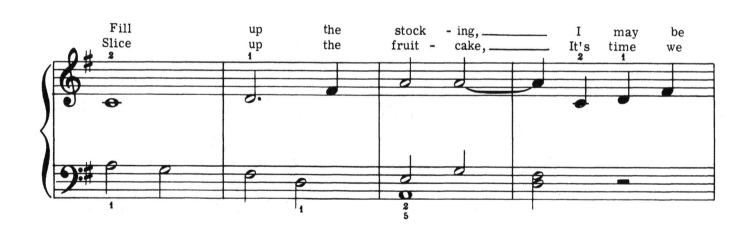

SILENT NIGHT

JOSEPH MOHR   FRANZ GRUBER